THE LIGHT IN YOUR EYES

LISA CASSMAN

Halo ●●●●
Publishing International

ISBN: 978-1-61244-304-1
Library of Congress Control Number: 2014912019

Printed in the United States of America

Published by Halo Publishing International
AP# 726
P.O. Box 60326
Houston, Texas 77205
Toll Free 1-877-705-9647
Website: www.halopublishing.com
E-mail: contact@halopublishing.com

CONTENTS

C h a p t e r   T h r e e :
FALLING IN LOVE — 41

C h a p t e r   F o u r :
GOODBYE — 63

*Introduction by the
Editor Leah Kelton*

Lisa and her husband Steve met as teenagers at summer camp 30 years ago.

The miles and circumstances kept them apart— so long that they both grew to adulthood, married, started families— but never completely forgot the kindness and hope they discovered in one another that summer so long before.

These poems were written by a teenage girl heartsick in love. And as a mature woman, heartbroken by a cruel and breaking-down marriage.

Every poem is either aching for him, terrified she won't have him, or gushingly thankful she'd had the grace of meeting him at all. From the first week as teens, to today as a gratefully married couple, brought back together years and lifetimes later by a loving heavenly Father, her poetry speaks of how thankful she is to be directed to all that is kind and good and gracious in this world, drawn by the light in his eyes.

Love

It's only a four letter word.

It's in the dictionary, it's in the Bible,

It's been in my heart for a long, long while.

Why is it, then, when I want to share my love,

It's not with someone special, only with a friend from above?

I want to give, but no one will receive

This love I have for all to see.

Take my love, and share with all.

But give me what I love best of all.

A kiss on the lips, a hand in mine

Will satisfy all, with a hug on the side.

Now one might say this is all a dream,

But the truth of the matter is quite frank, you'll see.

All needs love and all needs a hug,

That is me, please take care of my love.

By Steven K. Cassman

Chapter One

DREAMING

Have you ever had the opportunity to meet someone so special that you just know that someday you want to be with them? As a teenage girl at camp, this very good-looking young man came and invited me to the evening banquet they put on for the campers. No boy had ever invited me to be a part of something so special before, so I was beside myself and very much interested in joining him for this special evening.

I wanted so badly to be a part of his life, and the poems here, written during that time, show the inner feelings I knew then, aching for him to be a part of my life forever.

But our lives were so different— we lived many miles apart…

DREAMING

I'm thinking that someday my dream
May come true.
Will I ever really be with you?
That day when you hold
Me in your arms,
Never letting go!
I see that our lives are so different--
Living many miles apart-- and
It may not ever be.
Just remember:
You will always have a place with me,
If only in my heart.

When?

When will we be together?
Only time will tell.
The heartache I've caused,
The loneliness I feel…
Jealousy is a part
Of my feelings as well.

Can we ever be?
Maybe nothing but the memory.
I need to know how you feel.
I need to know if there's a hope
Of you taking the key
To my heart…

So Wrong

How could I have been so wrong
To think that we could ever be?
The times we were together
Were the best for me.
I only hurt myself
Trying to tell you
That I love you.
My only hope was to hear you say,
"I love you too."

Part Of You

Can I ever have the one I really love?
Will I be able to have your arms around me?
And hear you say, "I love you too"?
I won't take you for granted
And I will be true to you.
Please just let me in to your life, to be
Part of you.

Confusion

In my mind of confusion
I think of you a lot.
I don't understand why,
But the thoughts are always there.
The great friend you have been—
I can't even express
My gratitude, my thankfulness.
Will you come to me some day
And explain the feelings here?
I want you to hold me,
But I know you can't.
Could it be love that we are trying to hide?
Thanks again for listening
And for being the man you are.
Maybe someday we'll know
What is actually
Going on here.

Timing

When the timing is right
We will know how we feel.
The touching will come.
The kisses are rare.
I want you to hold me
And tell me you care.
Please walk to me
And don't let me go.

Body's Touch

I am feeling your warm, tender
Hands sliding down my body,
The smooth touch of your lips
Gently on mine, kissing so slowly,
Making my body tingle.
I can feel your arms around me
And you are holding my hands,
Not wanting to let go.
What could be greater than
To have our bodies
Touch and the warm feeling
Of you next to me?

Reality

I woke in the morning
Only to realize I've
Been dreaming all night.
You were there with me,
Holding me tight.
Here I was, not in reality,
Thinking maybe someday
It will happen to me.
Maybe we can be,
Just you and me.

One Wish

If I could have just one wish
I'd want it to be,
To tell you day after day how much
You mean to me.
Than you would put your arms
Around me, so I could feel free.
Will you hold me, and show you care?
Will you kiss me so gentle
And smooth?
Please let me tell you how much I love you.

EMBRACE

I can't control my feelings,
And this I know is true,
All my love and all my love,
I am giving them to you.
When you are around me,
I feel safe and cared for.
Knowing you are so close,
I don't want to let go.
Your kisses are so gentle
As you embrace me so.
This could only let me see
That you really care for me.
Are you in my dreams?
Or is this reality?

A Dream

I saw something I hadn't seen before:
A man who treats a woman with respect,
Has that special touch and loving smile,
Very understanding, and kind words said.
I like to see the light in his eyes,
Feel the touch of his gentle hands, and the
Softness of his lips. I like to hear
The honesty in his voice.
Could this just be a man in my dreams?

C h a p t e r   T w o

FRIENDSHIP

I was so excited when I was able to see him again the next year at summer camp.

As soon as I saw him, that feeling of safety and joy returned. It seemed like I had known him for many years and I felt like we could someday be best friends.

Steve and I spent a few years writing letters and talking on the phone, and the more we wrote, and talked, the more I liked him—there was just something about his heart. He was "real" and wanted to listen to what I had to say. I considered him a true friend, and out of that, started to fall in love with this man I felt so close to despite the miles between us. I never knew I could ever have a friend like him.

Our friendship helped me learn to like who I was, and I didn't want to take it for granted.

FRIENDSHIP

God will bring someone into our
Lives when we least expect it.
He brought to me a gentle,
Loving, listening friend;
Someone I can trust completely.
We both have grown in
Ways we didn't expect.
If I could take one thing from
Our friendship it would be:
"Thanks for showing me what a
Real friend is."

To You

This is a letter written to you
Letting you know I've been
Thinking things through.
I want to thank you for what you
Have done, and for who you
Have been.
Everything you have said—
You have shed a new light.
Now the tears come, wondering
If I can be as happy as I'd like
To be.
I feel like a burden, but please
Understand how much you
Mean to me.

When I Think Of All My Friendships

When I think of all the
Friendships I've had,
I end up being hurt.
As soon as I get close,
The door is shut on me.
This time I will watch my step,
As I know you will soon be gone—
You will see.
We feel so close when you listen.
I feel special because
You care.
I know you won't take
Me for granted.
You too, all the feelings you share.
I try not to let my feelings wonder,
Try not to walk away.
You mean so much to me,
In a very special way.

Missing You

When I have a friend like you,
I don't need much else--
Just your lasting love and your care.
I miss you more then you could ever know.
I pray God will bring you back to me
And let me have, once again, my friend
That I sure do miss.
Please come back and let me know you are okay.
I cry myself to sleep at night.
I think of you every waking moment.
Nobody can replace the memories
I had with you. I could tell you
Secrets never said to anyone.
If I could only have you in my life once again,
My life would be so complete.
I believe someday you will be back once more.

Special Touch

My greatest friendship I have known
Could only be with you.
My most joyous moments
Are with you, only you.
Please take my hand and never let it go…
Hold it tight as if you can't get away.
Could anything get in the way of our friendship so dear?
Could we keep the laughter going for years to come?
I need the special touch
I feel when you are with me.
Your tender heart and your smile are so warm to me.
You are the best friend I could have.

Thank You

Thank you for your friendship.
I'll cherish it through.
I've never met another
Man that compares to you.
You have a special listening ear,
You have made that known.
The words that you share
Come from your heart.
You know just what to say
To help me through life;
I couldn't get along without you.
Please don't ever leave me,
I need you as my friend.
Without you, I feel as if life would end.
Your words mean a lot,
Your eyes show they care.
Thanks again for the
Great friendship we do share.
Thank you for being a friend,
One whom I can talk to.
Please don't ever change,
Just keep on being you.

My life has changed

Since you've been around.

I can count on you when I am down.

You have shown to me

What a real friend is.

If you were to leave,

It is you I would miss.

FRIENDS

My friends come and go
And without them,
My life seems so slow.
As soon as we grow close,
They seem to be gone.
When will I have a friend forever?
I hope very soon,
As long as it is
NEVER!
Why did you have to leave?
You have been so much to me...
You are special, you're a listener,
But most of all, a friend.
I guess with all these words
I'd like to say
"Good-bye, I will miss you."

Not In A Million Years

I wipe the tears from my eyes,
Wondering what'll I do.
I said all the wrong words;
I hurt you more then I knew.

The trust won't be back.
Your heart can't forgive.
I have to learn to move on
And show that I can survive.

"I am sorry" won't help.
Now I am feeling hurt.
Please help me understand
So I can be more alert.

I wanted you to hold me,
To tell me I am yours,
I now know it won't happen,
Not in a million years.

Room In Our Hearts

We can wake with a smile
And start with a hug.
With the sun shining bright,
What can go wrong?
It could be little words said
Or something that was done.
"I'm sorry" may not do.
We need to find room
In our hearts to forgive,
And find love in there.

Words Are Stronger Than A Kiss

Words are stronger than a kiss;
Have more power than a hug.
You can feel comfort from a hug,
And feel loved by a kiss,
But words can damage the heart.

Deeper

I am not sure I can thank you enough
For the thoughtfulness you have shown.
Your friendship is such a precious
Gift to me.
If I need a shoulder to cry on I know
You are there to hold me.
If I need someone to laugh with me,
You are by my side.
I am not sure I can explain to you
Why I feel the way I do.
Thank you so much for your
Caring heart, and understanding
That my love for you is much deeper
Than anyone could imagine.

Time Will Tell

We take life for granted
We don't see it as it is
The time we spend here
Should be filled with happiness
We need one another
But we don't need to be hurt
Can we help each other
To keep alert?
You are a special friend
Some things we cannot have
I wish life was easier
And I could have you to love
Please understand I am confused
And I would like to be with you
But only time will tell
In everything we do.

Teen Love

Our eyes meet,
I look at him, he looks at me.
Talking, laughing, could this be?
Holding hands, hugging and then
WOW! The kiss.
Dates and "I love you"
Should be next.
Twisting, turning, knots so tight.
Love can be, yes it can.
I send a text, I wait and wait!
None returned, and my heart aches.
I go to school, then I know.
He's with someone else, here I go.
And then it happens… could it be?
Is it for real?
Our eyes meet…

Falling In Love

After that second summer at camp, I didn't get to see him again. We had spent time talking on the phone and writing letters, but that just wasn't enough for me. I knew I was falling in love and I really wanted to be with this guy. I wanted someone who liked me for who I was, not putting any judgment on me. Steve made me feel free to be me.

But because of the distance between us, and life moving forward, that summer was the last time we saw one another. Life just got too crazy .

The last time we spoke, he was in the army and stationed in Texas. We talked for quite a while, and after our conversation was over, I knew in my heart we could not be together. I didn't have the heart to tell him how much I had fallen in love with him.

Holding On Tight

It all started with one small date,
A lot of talking, and it got late.
Then what happened?
Was it something said?
As he looked in my eyes,
Our lips met.

It was a time of love,
And a time of passion.
Could this happen
To be our new fashion?
He held on to me tight!
It was at that moment I knew
What a wonderful guy he is!

Ways To Love You

I can think of hundreds of ways to
Love you.
Just to name a few:
The way you hold me
With your warm hands,
The way you look at me
With your beautiful blue eyes,
And tell me you love me.
You sing love songs softly into my ears,
Taking my hand as we walk in the wind,
The warm breeze calming our
Spirits…
Thank you for being in my life.

Like A Rose

If you were to give me a rose,
My love is just as real!
With a yellow rose,
It would shine just as brightly.
The petals are countless,
Just as the ways I love are endless.
If I had a plastic rose,
Just as my love for you will not die.
My love for you is just as wild
As the wildflowers in the fields.
If you had given me a red rose,
My heart is on fire when I am with you.
You are more beautiful than any rose.
And more pure than a white,
Sweet-smelling rose.

Tell Me That You Love Me

45

Please tell me you love me,
Please tell me you care!
Don't hold your feelings back,
Please say, "With you
My life I will share.
Please hold me tight,
Don't ever let me go.
You need me and
I need you, more than
You'll ever know."

ℒIFE...

Life would have been much easier if I
Could have stopped myself.
I didn't mean to love you,
It wasn't in my plan.
I had tried love once or twice before
And now things got out of hand.
So when you came along,
I thought this may be fun.
I didn't want to fall in love
With you or anyone!
I feel I have been tricked;
You have caught me unaware
By being so kind and wonderful,
And always being there.
It's really kind of fun,
The things you say and do!
Thanks for your kind heart,
And letting me be part of you!

Thinking Of You

When I think of you,
I think of a beautiful day.
I wake in the morning only to see
The sun shining in my window,
Just like seeing your face to brighten my day.
Or the softness of the rain is like the tenderness of
Your hands touching my hands, tingling all over.
I walk outside in the warm summer air only to
Remember the warmth of being around you,
Knowing that you care.
The singing of the birds could only be as listening to
Your voice echoing through my ears,
To hear the whistles of happy tunes.
The skies remind me of my love eternal,
It's never ending and will be here forever.
What about the beautiful flowers in bloom, with different
meanings to each one?
The same goes for my many loves for you,
Too numerous to mention,
When I remember your beauty.
As the moon reflects on a beautiful lake with stars all around,
I think of your smiling face and eyes lit up,

Our lips touching and bodies held together.

So when you wake in the morning, remember throughout
the day,

If nothing else seems right,

You, and only you, could be my shining light to brighten

My way.

So Right

I love you with all my heart,
It's been tough right from the start.
I look at you with tears in my eyes,
Wanting you to know that it's
No disguise.
My troubles come from deep within,
Along with that, I want to win.
Someday I'd like you to be mine.
Is it at all possible?
I would like to quit my crying.
I need you more now than I did before.
Each day I grow to love you more and more.
Can you understand you are
The most beautiful man I have met?
I need to feel that I have not lost yet.
I won't give up my fight, all because
I feel this is so right.

When I Look At You

When I look at you I can only see
The feelings I hide so deep inside.
I become afraid to open up,
Not knowing if you would
Understand.
Will you let me talk to you?
Will you stand by me
When I need you the most?
I have held on so long,
Not wanting to let go.
My heart feels so close to you,
And the love I feel just won't
Go away.

Thinking Of Love

Love is so beautiful, like the flowers
In the spring and the fall leaves
Blowing silently.
It could be sitting by a warm blazing
Fireplace on a cold winter's day.
Love is the look in your eyes when I gaze at you.
It is your beautiful smile, so wonderful and precious.
Love is looking past your faults and
Finding the best in you.
So when I think of love,
I think of all these things,
But most of all I think of you.

Thoughts Of You

Even on the darkest, cloudiest days,
Knowing you are around,
My day is full of sunshine
And not any pain.
My tears are like the rain,
Soft but gentle, watering
My wonderful thoughts of you.
Seeing you in the gentle breezes
Adds beauty in my dreams.
My thoughts of you will never go.
They are strong like the waves of the sea.

Looking At You

I look at you
Through your eyes;
Your beauty is within.
Your smile tells me a thousand
Words, and I just have to grin.
I have learned so much from you.
I realize now I have more in me.
I have so much to thank you for.
My love for you will never die.
I will remember you for years to come
Even if I have to move on.

All Along

The feelings have been there all along,
I just didn't know they were this strong.
They all came back to me
When I saw your eyes, you see.
"Please look forward; don't look back"
I told myself.
I feel there is love to share,
And I want you by my side.

Lifeless

When I saw you today
My body was lifeless.
You can charm any woman
Any time that you want.
Our lives are so different,
That's why we are apart.
I thought it was love, but
I guess I was wrong.
Do you care, or did you at all?
The memories are great,
But the timing was wrong.

Show Me

My love for you will never die,
My love for you will not fail.
So please tell me you love me,
And I will tell you the same.
I need to, whether by
Phone or by mail—
Just show me you care.

Love Is...

Being there with a listening ear,
Even when you don't want to hear it.
Being honest enough not to hurt
Yourself or the one you love.
Looking past faults of others
Knowing they are there
Going around them and not
Stepping on them.
Allowing your hands to be
Gentle enough to put goosebumps
On one's body while holding
And being held.
Being with you could only mean
Loving and being loved.

The Light In Your Eyes

The light in your eyes
Shines brighter than the sun.
The touch of your hands
Feels softer then the clouds.
I feel myself melting
When I think of your kiss.
That smile of yours is worth
A million dollars.
When you talk to me
I feel like dancing.
Just looking at you,
My heart is on fire.

Tonight

It's time to let you know
How I really feel.
The feelings I never even knew.
I even tried to tell myself
To stay away from you.
Please let me come in today
And let me hold you tight.
When the time is right,
You will see you will feel the same.
Maybe you are too blind
To see what is really there.
I want to feel it in your kiss
And to have it hold me tight.
I could just be dreaming…
Please wake me up tonight.

As The World Turns Round And Round

As the world turns round and round,
I want everyone to know what I have found.
Satan has been defeated in my life,
A life created by God!
I have the love I never knew—
God wants you to have it too.
He is at work behind closed doors.
Are you checking around?
It could be your neighbors!
What were you doing when they needed you?
Tell me now, what will you do?
They were lost and never told.
We had the chance—
Now they are left
In the cold!

Love Is...

Love is special
Love is warm
Love is understanding
Love is unconditional
Love waits…
I give my love to you!

GOODBYE

I was crushed knowing I would not be part of Steve's life. I had to force myself to let the feelings go. I had to say goodbye in my heart, realizing that there just wasn't room in our lives to tell him how I felt.

That phone call we had when he was station in Texas was the last contact I had with him, and saying goodbye was so hard to do…

Staying Strong

Saying goodbye is hard to do
I will never know if he loved me too
God, please give me strength to go on
It's hard to do, but I must be strong
Thank you, God, for your
Gift of love,
Your love that's cleansed me
and made me whole…
You will now have my heart

I Have To Say Goodbye

Just when I thought they were through,
All the feelings I had for you,
I come to realize they are still there.
Love is so strong—how could I have
Been so wrong?
I now know what I was feeling is so
True.
Many years later, I still think
Of you.
I have to say goodbye to what I had—
Please help me!
What should I do?
God is my stronghold and my
Number one love,
Only He can
Help me through what I feel.
With tears in my eyes,
I want to say goodbye.
Please remember, I love you so much.
You will always have a special
Place in my heart.

Good-Bye

It's now time to say good-bye;
Something I didn't want to do.
I guess I hadn't realized
You didn't love me too.
Please accept my apologies
And forgive my selfishness.
I was determined to have you;
To have you to myself.
I wanted you to have my heart,
And to hold me in your arms at night.
I wanted to hear you say to me
You wanted me as well.
It will be long and painful,
But I have to give you up.
It feels as if someone stole my heart
And threw it in the dump.
Please just promise me one thing:
That I can still be your friend.

Chapter Five

HURT

Taking all I had in me, I had to move on with my life. Over time, I grew up, married, started a family, and raised my handsome boys.

But my marriage was very dark. For many years I didn't like who I was because of the circumstances I found myself in. It was crushing to live through, and crushing to end.

It was a painful process, but God taught me to like myself again and accept myself for who He created me to be. I knew and believed that my life could be whole and happy again someday.

Hurt and exhausted, I didn't want a relationship again. I took life one day at a time.

Falling

One step at a time,
Walking,
Looking all around.
Falling on a rock, life has slipped
By me.
Driving down the dusty road,
The car getting dirty.
Still a losing
Battle.
Will I ever feel clean?
Chatting,
Others talking all around,
But no one will listen, I'm feeling lost
And all alone.
In line, for a latte--
Waiting as if
Life is standing still.
The faster I run, the more I gasp.
I can't breathe.
I finally picked myself up,
Wiped the dust off and no more
Standing still.

I move on, running
With pride, knowing I can breathe again.
No more letting life
Pass me by.

The Calm Before

Stop, think, breathe…
Boiling, bubbling, what's next?
Listen-- it sounds like thunder,
CRASH, BANG!
Too scared to move.
The door opens, then slams shut!
Quiet again, until
Next time!

Walking

Walking down the path,
Following the sand,
You start to sink.
At first you don't feel it,
Then faster, faster, faster
You are tumbling down.
You can't get control of your life.
In a moment's time, you are gone!

THE STORM

Thunder, lightening, rain.
Flashes all around.
Crashes, loud noises,
Hiding, keeping safe!
Is it done yet?

Lost

Feeling alone, abandoned, feeling fear.
When will this ache go away?
Nobody will listen, nobody cares.
Tell me I'm not crazy
And, someday, it will be okay.
I have tried, but still get hurt.
I want that hope, but it's just
Not here.
In the corner, crying;
The tears won't even come.
I have poured so many.
Someday soon, this will end.
The darkness shall turn to light.
Just when I feel the time is near,
It happens again, one more time.
Again and again!
Someone, please, tell this to
Go away. I want it all to end.
Still no one to talk to.
I feel so ashamed.
Now I am to blame; it's my fault.
I shouldn't have let this happen.
Soon, hopefully soon.

ʙBECAUSE

I finally found the "real" me.
When you ripped my heart in two,
You hurt me more than you knew.
I let go of all the aches and pains,
And moved on without you.
I now have the love I deserve,
To share with someone who
Truly cares and takes me
As I am.

Lies

You know the truth and where
It lies.
The darkness you hide within,
Your words don't mean a thing.
Have you not a care?
Why are you selfish?
What lies in between?
Sadness, blue, weakness, too.
Muscles tighten, hard to breathe,
Tears that flow, until there are no more.
Now you want to hold me?
NO! It is too late.
I am now strong enough to walk away.

God Is Love

God is my love
And my heart's desire;
I can count on Him to
Show me the way.
Are you troubled?
Are you afraid?
Be not, and strengthen
Yourself by His love.
Come to Him for a new life—
Leave the past to open
A new pure heart.
My desire is to follow Him
Please help me, Lord, to
Do your will!

BRIGHTER TIMES

As I learned to like myself once again, I knew I could again have someone special who loved me for who I was. I searched for my special friend—the one who had first taught me such love in his kindness. Not knowing what would happen with our friendship, all I wanted was to be speak again with that friend that listened to my words and heard what my heart really had to say.

After finding him, I felt the instant connection, and knew that the friendship was still there. This was the friend I had missed for many years.

As we talked and searched our hearts, we knew that we shared something special. We have now come together with a love that can't be torn apart.

He has helped me through so much and loves me for who I am.

I am so thankful that my best friend is now my husband.

You

Let me tell you how much I love you,
Let me tell you how much I care.
I need you arms around me--
I want your arms around me.
I would like to hear your voice.
Your friendship means a lot to me.
Thanks for your listening ear.
You're my best friend,
But most all, you are special just being you.

I Love You

You have given me so much.
You gave me your hands
To hold my tears,
Just when I thought there was no place
for them to go.
You gave me your ears to listen,
So I wouldn't fall apart.
You gave me your mouth for the
soft spoken words to let me know I would be okay.
But most of all you gave to me
Your heart to share with
Me when I thought I couldn't any more.
Mine was shattered, but now on the mend.
Thanks for sharing your life with me.
I love you!

Like Who Your Spouse Is

And like what they represent...
Thank you for being you, please don't ever change.
Your thoughtfulness is known in everything you do.
Everyone has their faults, I know you do too—
I just seem to see the best in everything you do.
I won't take you for granted; I like who you are.
I've taken time to know you, and it's you I like so far!

Together At Last

I now know you really care,
I guess I have known all along—
I was just too scared.
I see it in your eyes,
I feel it when you smile, and
Hear it in your voice.
Are you too blind to see our feelings?
I want to say "I love you,"
But I don't know how.
Someday we will be together.
Somehow the time will come
When we can't hide it
Anymore.

Special Moments

I think of you throughout the day
And the special moments we spend together.
I like when you open your heart to me,
I like to hear how you feel and what you are thinking.
Each time I am with you,
You mean more and more.
Nobody understands me like you do.
I love you for who you are,
And for what I am when I am with you.
We have so few precious things—
That's why there is just one of you!

CHOICES

Life gives us many choices.
I chose many years ago that I
Wanted to be with you someday.
I never let go of that feeling.
As the years went by
My heart grew stronger,
My love didn't fade away.
We both made choices that
Brought us in different directions,
And I will now finally get to
Tell you how I feel.
Thanks for being a part of my life.
The years were worth waiting through.
I love you!

REFLECTION

Looking back, I have made many choices,
Some, were great and some not so much.
No regrets, just moving forward.
God has given me peace and
I found a new me.
I feel I can now love the way it was meant to be.
The trust is real, the secrets no more.
When I look at you, your
Eyes are filled with love and
Bring forth a beautiful glow.
You have a great, sweet spirit
And allow me to be myself.
You were definitely worth waiting for,
And we are destined to be
Together forever.

CPSIA information can be obtained
at www.ICGtesting.com
Printed in the USA
FFOW02n2236070714
6260FF